C000082478

THIS BOOK BELONGS TO

_____

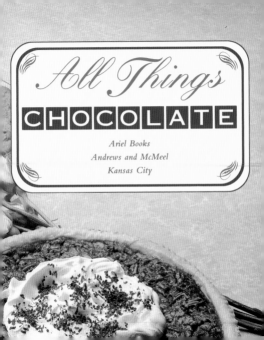

All Things
CHOCOLATE

Ariel Books

Andrews and McMeel

Kansas City

ISBN: 0-8362-3061-2

Library of Congress Catalog Card Number: 93-72651

Contents

Introduction

*F*ew treats are as cherished as chocolate. Whether milk, dark, or white, it is savored for dessert, for snacks, and for those times when we need a "little something special." Chocolate is for lovers, nestled in heart-shaped boxes. It's for children, molded into Easter bunnies or Santas or stirred into hot milk. It's proffered by houseguests to hosts and by dinner partners to one another, as well as by world-class hotels as a goodnight gesture to their patrons.

As universally loved as it may be, not all chocolate is created equal. The flavor and texture, and consequently the cooking properties, can vary greatly depending on how the particular chocolate is made. All chocolate, except white, contains chocolate liquor and added cocoa butter. What else it contains (lecithin, sugar, or milk solids) and the amount added affect the way the chocolate tastes and reacts when cooked. How the cocoa beans are processed into chocolate in the first place has a great deal to do with the quality of the chocolate, too.

Unsweetened chocolate is made from chocolate liquor, the substance extracted from the cocoa beans once the cocoa butter, or fat, is removed. During processing, the cocoa butter is put back until the finished product contains 50 percent or more cocoa butter. Unsweetened chocolate is most commonly sold in one-ounce squares in boxes holding eight ounces.

Semisweet and *bittersweet chocolate*, also called dark chocolate, are made from chocolate liquor, cocoa butter, sugar, and such flavorings as vanillin and vanilla. European dark chocolates most often are called bittersweet (although that is not categorically true), while American darks are referred to as semisweet. For the following recipes we used American semisweet chocolate, easily available in supermarkets in boxes containing eight one-ounce squares.

Milk chocolate is most commonly purchased for eating. It is made from chocolate liquor, cocoa butter, sugar, flavorings, and milk solids. The milk solids make this chocolate sensitive to heat, causing it to displace some chocolate liquor. Thus, it cannot be substituted for dark chocolate in recipes. In this book we used milk chocolate chips, sold at supermarkets alongside the more familiar semi-sweet chips.

White chocolate contains no chocolate liquor and therefore is not officially considered chocolate in the United States. It is a mixture of cocoa butter, milk solids, sugar, butterfat, lecithin, and flavorings. White chocolate is very sensitive to heat and difficult to cook with.

Cocoa powder is made from chocolate liquor from which most of the cocoa butter has been removed; however, it is not fat-free. Alkalized cocoa, also called Dutch process, is treated with an alkali to produce a milder-flavored cocoa. Nonalkalized cocoa is lighter in color but has a stronger flavor. In the following recipes we used nonalkalized cocoa made by a major American manufacturer. Be careful to buy *unsweetened* cocoa powder.

Chocolate Cakes

*W*hether frosted with a deep dark chocolate or a bright white icing, or rolled around a luscious mocha cream, chocolate cake is a universal favorite. Ask almost anyone what flavor cake she or he prefers, and the answer invariably will be "chocolate!" Made for a birthday, dinner party, family get-together, or holiday, a chocolate cake is indescribably satisfying.

CHOCOLATE LAYER CAKE

- 2¼ cups all-purpose flour
- 1½ tsp. baking soda
- 1 tsp. baking powder
- ½ tsp. salt
- 1 Tbl. lemon juice
- 1½ tsp. vanilla extract
- 1 cup milk
- 3 oz. unsweetened chocolate, coarsely chopped
- ½ cup boiling water
- 12 Tbl. softened butter
- 2 cups sugar
- 3 large eggs
  Fluffy Chocolate Frosting (pg. 18)

Preheat the oven to 350°F. Grease two 9" round cake pans. Dust them with flour and tap out the excess.

Whisk together the flour, baking soda, baking powder, and salt. Set aside.

Stir the lemon juice and vanilla into the milk and set aside.

Put the chopped chocolate in a bowl and pour the boiling water over it. Let sit for 30 seconds. Stir until the chocolate melts.

Cream the butter and sugar until light and fluffy. Add the eggs, one at a time, beating after each one.

Add the melted chocolate and beat until blended.

Alternate beating the flour mixture and milk mixture into the chocolate mixture, beginning and ending with the flour.

Scrape the batter equally into the pans and bake for 20 to 25 minutes, until the layers pull away from the sides of the pans. Let cool in the pans for 5 minutes and then turn onto wire racks. When the layers are cool, spread with Fluffy Chocolate Frosting.

Serves 8 to 10.

FLUFFY CHOCOLATE FROSTING

10 Tbl. softened butter
4 cups confectioners' sugar
3 oz. unsweetened chocolate, melted and cooled
6 to 7 Tbl. heavy cream
2 tsp. vanilla extract

Cream the butter until light and fluffy. Lower the speed and add the sugar, a cup at a time, mixing until blended.

Add the chocolate and cream and beat well. Add the vanilla. Increase the speed and beat for 3 to 4 minutes until the frosting is fluffy and a good spreading consistency.   *Makes about 3 cups.*

DEVIL'S FOOD CAKE

- 2¼ cups all-purpose flour
- ½ cup unsweetened cocoa powder
- 1½ tsp. baking soda
- 1 tsp. baking powder
- 1 tsp. salt
- 8 Tbl. softened butter
- 1½ cups sugar
- ½ cup packed dark brown sugar
- 3 large eggs
- ¾ cup milk
- ½ cup water
- 1 tsp. vanilla extract
- Sour Cream Frosting (pg. 23)

Preheat the oven to 350°F. Grease two 9" round cake pans. Dust them with flour and tap out the excess.

Whisk together the flour, cocoa, baking soda, baking powder, and salt. Set aside.

Cream the butter and both sugars until light and fluffy. Add the eggs, one at a time, beating after each one.

Combine the milk, water, and vanilla. Alternate beating the flour mixture and milk mixture into the butter mixture, beginning and ending with the flour.

Scrape the batter equally into the pans and bake for 30 to 35 minutes, until the layers pull away from the sides of the pans. Let cool in the pans for 5 minutes and then turn onto wire racks. When the layers are cool, spread with Sour Cream Frosting.

Serves 8 to 10.

SOUR CREAM FROSTING

- ¾ cup sour cream
- 5 Tbl. softened butter
- 2 tsp. vanilla extract
- 4 cups confectioners' sugar

Cream the sour cream and butter until light and fluffy. Add the vanilla and beat well. Reduce the speed. Add the confectioners' sugar, a cup at a time, beating after each addition until smooth. Refrigerate for at least 1 hour to thicken. *Makes about 2½ cups.*

CHOCOLATE ROLL

- ⅔ cup all-purpose flour
- ⅓ cup unsweetened cocoa powder
- ¼ tsp. salt
- 5 large eggs
- 1 cup sugar
- 4 Tbl. butter, melted and cooled
- 1½ tsp. vanilla extract
- 3 Tbl. unsweetened cocoa powder, for sprinkling
- Mocha Cream (pg. 27)

Preheat the oven to 350°F. Grease a 17" × 11" jelly roll pan. Dust with flour and tap out the excess.

Whisk together the flour, cocoa, and salt. Set aside. Whisk together the eggs and sugar. Set the bowl over a pan of simmering water and whisk for 3 to 4 minutes until the mixture is lukewarm. Remove from the water and beat at high speed for 2 to 3 minutes until thick and frothy.

Fold the flour mixture into the egg mixture, a little at a time. Do not overmix. Fold in the butter and vanilla.

Scrape the batter into the pan. Bake for 15 to 20 minutes, until the cake pulls away from the sides of the pan. Let the cake cool slightly in the pan.

Dust a clean, dry kitchen towel with about 2 tablespoons of cocoa. Invert the cake onto the towel. Sprinkle the cake with the remaining tablespoon of cocoa. Beginning at the short end, roll the cake into a tight roll inside the towel. Set aside to cool completely.

When it's completely cool, unroll the cake, lift it from the towel, and set it on a work surface. Spread Mocha Cream over the cake, leaving a 1" border. Roll the cake again and set, seam side down, on a serving platter.

Serves 8 to 10.

MOCHA CREAM

- 1 cup heavy cream
- 1 Tbl. sugar
- 1 Tbl. unsweetened cocoa
  powder
- ½ tsp. vanilla extract
- 1 Tbl. brewed coffee, cooled

Beat the cream in a chilled bowl until very soft peaks begin to form. Add the sugar, cocoa, and vanilla and beat just until incorporated. Add the coffee and beat until soft, spreadable peaks form.

Makes about 2 cups.

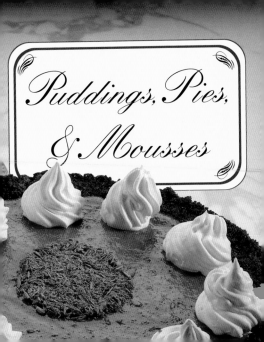

*R*ich chocolate cream pie has a lot in common with creamy chocolate pudding. They share velvety consistencies and special places in our hearts as ultimate comfort foods. Add to these two a sweet pecan pie, a minty variation of chocolate pudding, and an indulgent chocolate mousse, and you have a collection of desserts that is sure to please the most demanding chocolate lover.

CHOCOLATE PUDDING

- ¾ cup milk
- 1¼ cups half-and-half
- ½ cup sugar
- 2 Tbl. cornstarch
  Pinch salt
- 3 large egg yolks, lightly beaten
- 3 oz. semisweet chocolate,
  finely chopped
- 2 tsp. vanilla extract
  Whipped cream, for garnish

Combine the milk, half-and-half, sugar, cornstarch, and salt in a saucepan. Heat for 2 to 3 minutes, whisking, until hot but not boiling. Remove from the heat.

Gradually stir ¼ cup of the hot milk mixture into the egg yolks. Combine the egg yolks with the rest of the hot milk. Heat again, whisking, for 5 to 6 minutes until thick but not boiling.

Pour the hot mixture over the chopped chocolate, let sit for 30 seconds, and whisk until the chocolate melts. Cool for 10 to 15 minutes. Add the vanilla and whisk to combine.

Pour the pudding into four 6-oz. custard cups. Press plastic wrap directly on the surface of each cup and let cool to room temperature. Refrigerate for 3 to 4 hours or overnight. Garnish with whipped cream.   *Serves 4.*

MINTED CHOCOLATE PUDDING

- ¾ cup milk
- 1¼ cups half-and-half
- ½ cup sugar
- 2 Tbl. cornstarch
  Pinch salt
- 3 large egg yolks, lightly beaten
- 3 oz. semisweet chocolate,
  finely chopped
- 2 tsp. mint extract
  Fresh mint leaves, for garnish
  Whipped cream, for garnish

Combine the milk, half-and-half, sugar, cornstarch, and salt in a saucepan. Heat for 2 to 3 minutes, whisking, until hot but not boiling.

Gradually stir ¼ cup of the hot milk mixture into the egg yolks. Combine the egg yolks with the rest of the hot milk. Heat again, whisking, for 5 to 6 minutes until thick but not boiling.

Pour the hot mixture over the chopped chocolate, let sit for 30 seconds, and whisk until the chocolate melts. Cool for 10 to 15 minutes. Add the mint extract and whisk to combine.

Pour the pudding into four 6-oz. custard cups. Press plastic wrap directly on the surface of each cup and let cool to room temperature. Refrigerate for 3 to 4 hours or overnight. Garnish with mint leaves and whipped cream.

Serves 4.

OLD-FASHIONED CHOCOLATE CREAM PIE

Chocolate Cookie
Crust (pg. 41)

- 1½ cups milk
- 1½ cups half-and-half
- ¾ cup sugar
- 3 Tbl. cornstarch
- 2 Tbl. all-purpose flour
  Pinch salt
- 4 egg yolks, lightly beaten
- 4 oz. semisweet chocolate,
  finely chopped
- 2 tsp. vanilla extract
  Whipped cream, for garnish

Combine the milk, half-and-half, sugar, cornstarch, flour, and salt in a saucepan. Heat for 2 to 3 minutes, whisking, until hot but not boiling. Remove from the heat.

Gradually stir ¼ cup of the hot milk mixture into the egg yolks. Combine the egg yolks with the rest of the hot milk. Heat again, whisking, for 6 to 7 minutes until thick but not boiling.

Pour the hot mixture over the chopped chocolate, let sit for 30 seconds, and whisk until the chocolate melts. Cool for 10 to 15 minutes. Add the vanilla and whisk to combine.

Pour the filling into the baked Chocolate Cookie Crust shell. Press plastic wrap directly on the surface and let cool to room temperature. Refrigerate for 3 to 4 hours or overnight. Garnish with whipped cream.

Serves 8 to 10.

CHOCOLATE COOKIE CRUST

1¾ cups crushed plain
       chocolate cookie wafers
8 Tbl. butter, melted

Preheat the oven to 300°F.

Finely grind the cookies in a food processor. Add the melted butter and pulse just until the mixture is moist. Press the mixture into a 9" pie plate.

Bake for about 10 minutes. Do not overbake; the crust should be slightly soft. Cool completely on a wire rack until firm. *Makes one 9" crust.*

CHOCOLATE PECAN PIE

Pie Dough (pg. 44)
4 large eggs
1 cup light corn syrup
¾ cup packed dark brown sugar
4 Tbl. butter, melted and cooled
2 tsp. vanilla extract
1 cup coarsely chopped pecans
1 cup semisweet chocolate chips
Whipped cream or vanilla ice cream (optional)

Preheat the oven to 350°F.

Make Pie Dough and roll it out on a lightly floured surface to about ⅛" thick. Press it into a 9" pie plate, leaving about ½" overhang. Refrigerate.

Beat the eggs until frothy. Add the corn syrup, sugar, melted butter, and vanilla. Beat well until the sugar dissolves. Stir in the pecans.

Take the pie shell from the refrigerator and sprinkle the chocolate chips in the bottom. Pour the pecan batter into the pie shell. Trim the edges of the pastry and crimp with a fork.

Bake for 40 to 50 minutes until the filling is set. Cool completely on a wire rack. Serve with whipped cream or ice cream, if desired. *Serves 8 to 10.*

PIE DOUGH

1 cup all-purpose flour
½ tsp. salt
3 Tbl. chilled butter, cut up
3 Tbl. chilled vegetable
    shortening, cut up
2 to 3 Tbl. ice water

Mix the flour and salt and then add
the butter and shortening. Use two
knives or your fingertips to blend until
the mixture resembles coarse crumbs.

Sprinkle the ice water, a tablespoon
at a time, over the flour mixture,
tossing until the dough comes

together. Gather the dough into a ball and wrap in plastic. Refrigerate the dough for at least 1 hour or for up to 2 days. *Makes one single crust for a 9" pie.*

NOTE: To freeze an unbaked pie shell, press the pastry into a freezer-safe pie plate and crimp the edges. Wrap it first in plastic and then in two layers of foil. Freeze the pie shell for up to one month. When ready to use, take it from the freezer and fill it. Bake the pie as directed in the recipe—no need to adjust the baking times.

CHOCOLATE MOUSSE

- 3 Tbl. milk
- 2 Tbl. sugar
- 1 Tbl. brewed coffee
- 6 oz. semisweet chocolate,
  coarsely chopped
- 2 Tbl. softened butter,
  cut into pieces
- 2 tsp. vanilla extract
- 1 cup heavy cream

Combine the milk, sugar, and coffee
in a saucepan. Heat for 2 to 3 minutes,
whisking, until boiling. Pour over the

chopped chocolate. Let sit for 30 seconds, then whisk until smooth.

Whisk in the butter, a piece at a time. Add the vanilla and whisk to combine. Let the mixture cool completely.

Beat the cream in a chilled bowl until soft peaks begin to form. Fold a little cream into the chocolate mixture and then fold this mixture into the rest of the whipped cream. Spoon the mousse into four 6-oz. custard cups. Cover each cup with plastic wrap and chill for 2 to 3 hours or overnight.

Serves 4.

Brownies &
Blondies

Brownies are all-American inventions, capturing the imagination of a nation that likes to do good things in big ways. They offer mouthfuls of intense chocolate flavor and will immediately quell all chocolate cravings—for a little while! We offer classic nut-filled brownies, a double-chocolate extravaganza, heavenly brownies laced with peanut butter, and blondies with more chocolate chips studding every bar than you may have thought possible!

CHOCOLATE PEANUT BUTTER BROWNIES

- ½ cup all-purpose flour
- 1 Tbl. unsweetened cocoa powder
- Pinch salt
- ½ cup creamy peanut butter
- 4 Tbl. softened butter
- ½ cup plus 1 Tbl. sugar
- ½ cup packed light brown sugar
- 2 large eggs
- 1 tsp. vanilla extract
- ½ cup coarsely chopped unsalted peanuts
- 1 cup semisweet chocolate chips

Preheat the oven to 350°F. Grease an 8" square pan.

Whisk together the flour, cocoa, and salt. Set aside.

Cream the peanut butter and butter until light and fluffy. Add both sugars and cream until well blended. Add the eggs, one at a time, and beat until blended. Add the vanilla and beat well. Add the flour mixture and stir until incorporated.

Stir the peanuts and ½ cup of the chocolate chips into the batter. Scrape the batter into the pan. Bake for 30 to 35 minutes until firm. Remove from

the oven and sprinkle the remaining
½ cup of chocolate chips over the top
of the hot brownies. Let them sit for
about 1 minute. Spread the softened
chocolate over the brownies. Cool
completely in the pan set on a wire
rack.   *Makes 16 brownies.*

CLASSIC CHOCOLATE PECAN BROWNIES

- 2 oz. unsweetened chocolate, coarsely chopped
- 8 Tbl. butter
- 1 cup sugar
- 2 large eggs
- 1 tsp. vanilla extract
- ¾ cup all-purpose flour
  Pinch salt
- 1 cup coarsely chopped pecans

Preheat the oven to 350°F. Grease an 8" square pan.

Melt the chocolate and butter in the top of a double boiler over hot water. Stir until smooth. Remove from the heat and cool slightly.

Add the sugar and eggs. Whisk until well blended. Whisk in the vanilla.

Add the flour and salt and stir until blended. Stir the pecans into the batter.

Scrape the batter into the pan and bake for 25 to 30 minutes until a toothpick inserted in the center comes out with a few moist crumbs. Cool in the pan set on a wire rack.

Makes 16 brownies.

DOUBLE-CHOCOLATE BROWNIES

- 2 oz. unsweetened chocolate, coarsely chopped
- 8 Tbl. butter
- 1 cup sugar
- 2 large eggs
- 1 tsp. vanilla extract
- ¾ cup all-purpose flour
  Pinch salt
- ⅔ cup milk chocolate chips

Preheat the oven to 350°F. Grease an 8" square pan.

Melt the chocolate and butter in the

top of a double boiler over hot water. Stir until smooth. Remove from the heat and cool slightly.

Add the sugar and eggs. Whisk until well blended. Whisk in the vanilla.

Add the flour and salt and stir until blended. Stir ⅓ cup of the milk chocolate chips into the batter.

Scrape the batter into the pan. Sprinkle the remaining milk chocolate chips over the top. Bake for 25 to 30 minutes, until a toothpick inserted in the center comes out with a few moist crumbs. Cool in the pan set on a wire rack. *Makes 16 brownies.*

CHOCOLATE CHIP BLONDIES

- 8 Tbl. softened butter
- 1½ cups packed light brown sugar
- 2 large eggs
- 1 tsp. vanilla extract
- 1½ cups all-purpose flour
- 1 tsp. baking powder
- Pinch salt
- 1¼ cups semisweet chocolate chips

Preheat the oven to 350°F. Grease an 8" square pan.

Cream the butter and sugar until light and fluffy. Add the eggs, one at a time, and beat to blend. Add the vanilla and beat well.

Whisk together the flour, baking powder, and salt. Add to the batter and stir just until combined. Stir in the chocolate chips.

Scrape the batter into the pan and bake for 25 to 30 minutes, until a toothpick inserted in the center comes out with a few moist crumbs. Cool in the pan set on a wire rack.

Makes 16 blondies.

Cookies

Chocolate cookies make terrific cookie-jar treats. Ours are big and chewy, packed with rich chocolaty flavor guaranteed to satisfy hungry after-school munchers as well as more adult cookie hounds. From lovable chocolate chip cookies to fudgy chocolate drops and oatmeal cookies bursting with chocolate chips, these confections will make the cookie jar the favorite spot in the house.

CLASSIC CHOCOLATE CHIP COOKIES

2½ cups all-purpose flour
1 tsp. baking soda
¼ tsp. salt
8 Tbl. softened butter
1 cup sugar
½ cup packed dark brown sugar
2 large eggs
2 tsp. vanilla extract
2 cups semisweet chocolate chips
1 cup chopped walnuts

Preheat the oven to 375°F. Grease two baking sheets.

Whisk together the flour, baking soda, and salt. Set aside. Cream the butter and sugars until light and fluffy. Add the eggs, one at a time, and beat until blended. Add the vanilla and beat well. Add the flour mixture, a little at a time, and beat until blended. Stir in the chocolate chips and walnuts.

Drop the dough in rounded teaspoonfuls onto the baking sheets, leaving about 2" between them. Bake for 8 to 10 minutes until set. Cool for about 1 minute on the baking sheets and then cool completely on wire racks. *Makes 45 to 48 cookies.*

FUDGE DROPS

   1½ cups all-purpose flour
   ⅓ cup unsweetened cocoa powder
   ½ tsp. salt
   ¼ tsp. baking soda
   2 cups semisweet chocolate chips
  10 Tbl. softened butter
   1 cup packed light brown sugar
   ½ cup sugar
   2 large eggs
   1 tsp. vanilla extract

Preheat the oven to 375°F.

Whisk together the flour, cocoa, salt, and baking soda. Set aside. Finely chop the chocolate chips.

Cream the butter and sugars until light and fluffy. Add the eggs, one at a time, and beat until blended. Add the vanilla and beat well. Add the flour mixture, a little at a time, and beat until blended. Stir in the chocolate chips.

Using a spoon or your fingers, shape the dough into 1½" rounds. Place them on ungreased baking sheets at least 2" apart. Flatten each one slightly with the back of a spoon or your thumb. Bake for 6 to 8 minutes until firm.

Cool for about a minute on the baking sheets and then cool completely on wire racks. *Makes 36 to 40 cookies.*

OATMEAL CHOCOLATE CHIP COOKIES

- 3 cups rolled oats
- 1 cup all-purpose flour
- ½ tsp. baking soda
  Pinch salt
- 12 Tbl. softened butter
- 1¼ cups packed light brown sugar
- 2 large eggs
- 2 tsp. vanilla extract
- 1¼ cups semisweet chocolate chips

Preheat the oven to 375°F. Grease two baking sheets.

Whisk together the oats, flour, baking soda, and salt. Set aside.

Cream the butter and sugar until light and fluffy. Add the eggs, one at a time, and beat until blended. Add the vanilla and beat to blend. Add the flour mixture, a little at a time, and beat until blended. Stir in the chocolate chips.

Drop the dough in rounded teaspoonfuls onto the baking sheets, about 2" apart. Bake for 10 to 12 minutes until set. Cool for about 1 minute on the baking sheets and then cool completely on wire racks.

Makes 25 to 30 cookies.

Sauces & Drinks

Simple preparations sometimes are the best. Smooth chocolate sauce and rich hot fudge sauce turn an ordinary bowl of ice cream or a slice of pound cake into something special. And when you need a little extra nurturing, nothing beats a mug of creamy hot chocolate or hot mocha on a chilly, stormy morning or a tall, cool milkshake on a muggy afternoon.

CHOCOLATE SAUCE

½ cup half-and-half
½ cup milk
1 Tbl. sugar
8 oz. semisweet chocolate,
   coarsely chopped

Heat the half-and-half, milk, and sugar over medium-high heat until very hot but not boiling. Stir occasionally. Pour it over the chopped chocolate and let stand for about 30 seconds. Stir until smooth. Serve warm or cold. *Makes about 1½ cups.*

HOT FUDGE SAUCE

- ½ cup water
- 2 Tbl. butter
- 3 oz. unsweetened chocolate, coarsely chopped
- ¾ cup sugar
- 3 Tbl. light corn syrup
- Pinch salt
- 1½ tsp. vanilla extract

Heat the water and butter over medium heat until the butter melts. Remove from the heat and add the chopped chocolate. Let stand for 30 seconds. Stir until smooth.

Stir the sugar, corn syrup, and salt into the chocolate mixture. While stirring, heat again until boiling. Reduce the heat and simmer, stirring, for about 2 minutes. Remove from the heat. Cool for 3 to 4 minutes. Stir in the vanilla. Serve hot or warm.

Makes about 1¾ cups.

OLD-TIME HOT CHOCOLATE

- 1 cup milk
- 1 Tbl. sugar
- 2 tsp. unsweetened cocoa powder
- ½ tsp. vanilla extract (optional)
  Whipped cream, for garnish
  (optional)

Combine the milk, sugar, cocoa, and vanilla in a saucepan. While stirring, heat until hot but not boiling. Pour into a mug and garnish with whipped cream, if desired. *Serves 1.*

HOT MOCHA

- ½ cup milk
- 1 Tbl. sugar
- 2 tsp. unsweetened cocoa powder
- ½ cup brewed coffee, hot
  Whipped cream, for garnish
  (optional)

Combine the milk, sugar, and cocoa
in a saucepan. While stirring, heat
until hot but not boiling. Mix the hot
chocolate with the hot coffee in a mug.
Garnish with whipped cream, if
desired. *Serves 1.*

SUPER
CHOCOLATE
MILKSHAKE

1½ cups chocolate ice cream
⅓ cup cold milk
⅓ cup chocolate syrup

Combine the ice cream, milk, and syrup in a blender or food processor. Blend for about 1 minute until smooth and creamy. Pour into two tall glasses. Serve with straws. *Serves 2.*

The text of this book was set in

COPPERPLATE 31AB

AND BEMBO

by Beth Tondreau Design

of New York, NY.

BOOK DESIGN BY

Beth Tondreau Design/

Amy Donaldson